DK

I AM A ROYAL RULEBREAKER

WOMEN WHO SHAPED HISTORY

FERN RIDDELL

Illustrated by
Taylor Dolan

CONTENTS

FOREWORD ———— 4

ROYAL RULES ———— 6

ARTEMISIA I ———— 8
The pirate queen who killed a king

CLEOPATRA ———— 10
The queen who rocked a double identity as both Greek and Egyptian

BOUDICA ———— 12
The queen who destroyed entire cities

DAMSELS BE DAMNED ———— 14
Royal women who bested others in battle

PINGYANG ———— 16
The princess who raised an army to save her father

ÆTHELFLÆD ———— 18
The queen who defended her home from the Vikings

ARWA AL-SULAYHI ———— 22
The queen who stopped at nothing to avenge her family

MATILDA ———— 26
The woman who wouldn't take "no" for an answer

SUCCESSION SHAKERS ———— 28
Royal women who tried to take the throne

ELEANOR OF AQUITAINE ———— 30
The queen who ruled two nations

JOAN OF FLANDERS ———— 34
The woman who went into battle to get her husband back

ISABELLA D'ESTE ———— 36
The smart socialite who took the lead when needed

SCENE STEALERS ———— 38
Royal women who worked to shape the world

SAYYIDA AL-HURRA __ 40
The pirate queen who ruled the seas

THE RANI DURGAVATI _____ 44
The tiger hunter who rode an elephant into battle

ELIZABETH I _____ 48
The queen who would not wed

NOT TYING THE KNOT _____ 52
Royal women who chose to stay single

CHRISTINA OF SWEDEN _____ 54
The woman who dressed like a man

CATHERINE I _____ 58
The peasant who became a queen

ISABELLA OF PARMA 60
The great writer who lived in secret

LEADING LADIES ____ 62
Royal women who stole the spotlight

VICTORIA _____ 64
The queen who knew her own mind

CIXI _____ 66
The woman who may have poisoned her way into power

YAA ASANTEWAA ___ 70
The woman who went from farmer to fighter

SĀLOTE TUPOU III ____ 74
The queen who survived death twice

GLOSSARY AND INDEX _____ 78

ACKNOWLEDGEMENTS 80

SOUND THE TRUMPETS! WAVE YOUR BANNERS HIGH, PUT ON YOUR ARMOUR, DRAW YOUR WEAPONS, AND –

Wait a minute... Isn't this a book about princesses? Queens? Empresses?

Aren't they supposed to sit safely out of the way in high castles, protected from all the danger and just waiting to be rescued? Or be busy marrying boring, old men and pretending they've never heard of an education?

Maybe that's all a princess can do in old-fashioned fairy tales, but in the real world, royal women throughout history have done everything they can to misbehave. Until very recently, women had little power over their own lives. Most of the time, kings, fathers, brothers, and husbands made their decisions for them. Who they could marry, where they would live, what they could wear: all these were choices women did not get to make.

Imagine never being allowed to leave the house, or forced to marry someone you didn't love. Or – even worse – being made to leave home when you were just a child, and traded to a foreign country in a political deal! This was the reality many royal women were born into. Being a princess was not fun.

Here are some of the things many royal women were NOT allowed to do:
- ★ wear trousers
- ★ lead armies
- ★ start rebellions
- ★ be pirates
- ★ love who they wanted
- ★ study what they wanted
- ★ refuse to marry anyone at all, ever (and live alone with their cats)

But – from ancient Egyptian pharaohs and pirate queens, to great thinkers, trendsetters, and military commanders – many royal women have refused to submit to the stupid rules the world gave them.

Every entry in this book showcases the story of a real royal rulebreaker. Travel through thousands of years of history, all across the world, with these tales of brilliant, bold, and fearless women who made it all happen.

Where do you want to go first? Into a vicious sea-battle with the ferocious Artemisia? Or perhaps to climb up to the mountain fortress of the brave Rani Durgavati? Why not fight for independence with the courageous Yaa Asantewaa? Or become a patron of the arts with the gracious Isabella d'Este?

I want you to see just how confident and brave these royal rulebreakers were, whether they were defending their homes, writing radical pamphlets about how to make the world a better place, or just totally refusing to give up their power to anyone else.

They are rebellious, revolutionary, and sometimes really ruthless. Icons or tyrants – you decide! But, either way, without them our history would be very, very boring. So let's see what happens when princesses, queens, and empresses decide to break the rules...

DR FERN RIDDELL

ROYAL RULES

The way royal women were treated has changed across time and around the world. Whenever and wherever they came from, the mighty monarchs in this book have had many legal, social, and religious restrictions to rebel against!

FROM THE ANCIENT WORLD...

In prehistory – before the written word and central heating – many women held powerful positions as leaders and warriors. But as the ancient world expanded, men decided that women should not vote or get involved in politics, and that freedom and independence were something only men should have. Typical!

Centuries later, in many parts of the world, religion governed how lots of people lived. Most of the dominant religions treated men and women differently. They believed that a woman's place was in the home, and that she shouldn't care about much other than having babies. A lot of women secretly thought this was stupid. They wanted to be artists, philosophers, and leaders, too.

In Europe, after a long period of being told that women should be seen and not heard, new philosophies and ideas began to sprout – bringing brand new opportunities for women to break the rules. They could now be patrons, writers, and great thinkers. But many men still believed that a woman shouldn't be allowed to have the same rights as them, even if she was a powerful queen.

Flash forwards hundreds of years and welcome to the fight for women's rights! Where new technologies were being created, and science and art bloomed, women began to be fed up of being stuck in the shadows. They wanted to be part of the world, and stop having men take the credit for their great discoveries. "Votes for Women" became their new battle cry.

Throughout the twentieth century, women across the world began to get the right to vote for the first time. Laws were passed to guarantee women's freedom and independence. However, royal women were still expected to follow social customs and do what they were told. The new freedoms of ordinary women didn't really apply to princesses!

...TO TODAY

Many royal women still live by the old-fashioned ideas of the past, and are expected never to break the rules. But some of them have fought back, refusing to marry and becoming great patrons of the arts instead. They have used their royal power to make people pay attention to important charities and organizations, and to bring about change in the world.

As waves crashed around her, and the cries of seagulls filled the air, Artemisia I of Caria leapt onboard one of her five famous fighting ships, ready for battle.

FIGHTING SPIRIT

In her part of the ancient world, Artemisia broke all the rules. Women were supposed to stay home, they couldn't vote, and they certainly weren't allowed to fight. But Artemisia had other ideas. Instead, she became a pirate, commanding the most dangerous and feared fleet of ships in the Aegean Sea.

Artemisia ruled a beautiful city on the coast called Halicarnassus (modern-day Bodrum in Turkey). She was a powerful ally of the great Persian king, Xerxes I, who ruled over a vast empire spanning Iran, Egypt, and Iraq. But Xerxes was greedy for more. He wanted to rule over ancient Greece as well.

QUEEN OF THE WAVES

In 480 BCE, Xerxes tried to invade Greece, sailing his mighty army across the sea. Artemisia wouldn't let Xerxes go into battle alone. She took five of her deadliest pirate ships to join him, crewed by brave bands of soldiers, and led the ships herself – a bold choice for a woman of the time. The ancient Greeks were so angry that they offered their naval captains the huge reward of 10,000 drachmas if they managed to capture Artemisia alive.

c. 480 BCE
ARTEMISIA I
THE PIRATE QUEEN WHO KILLED A KING

But Artemisia was clever. She kept Greek flags onboard her ship, and whenever the ancient Greeks thought they had found her, she took down her flags for Halicarnassus and Xerxes and raised Greek flags in their place! This disguise fooled her enemies and saved her from capture many times.

ON THE RAMPAGE

The ancient Greeks were right to fear her. Sailing into the heart of the fight at the Battle of Salamis, Artemisia killed King Damasithymos – a man she was thought to have hated, even though he was one of her allies – by ramming his ship so hard that it sank. Even though she had attacked the wrong side, Xerxes was so impressed by Artemisia's bravery that he proudly presented her with a full suit of armour to show everyone what a mighty warrior she was.

c.70 BCE–30 BCE

CLEOPATRA

THE QUEEN WHO ROCKED A DOUBLE IDENTITY AS BOTH GREEK AND EGYPTIAN

Cleopatra didn't want to share ancient Egypt's throne with her little brother, Ptolemy XIII, so she fought to take Egypt for herself.

READY TO RULE

Born in Alexandria, Cleopatra was part of the ancient Greek family who ruled Egypt as the Ptolemaic dynasty. She was the first in her family to learn Egyptian, and her intellect didn't end there. She also spoke Greek, Hebrew, Latin, and the ancient languages of Syria and Iran!

When her father, Ptolemy XII, died, he named Cleopatra as his heir so she could become the next pharaoh. But he also expected her to marry her little brother and share the throne with him. Cleopatra hated this idea.

FRIENDS IN HIGH PLACES

To bolster her claim to the throne, Cleopatra looked for allies. She convinced the leader of the Roman Empire, Julius Caesar, to support her, and their army defeated Ptolemy XIII at the Battle of the Nile. Now Cleopatra could rule Egypt on her own and as she wished.

Back in Rome, Julius Caesar was assassinated by a group that included his so-called friend, Marc Antony. But this wasn't bad news for Cleopatra, as Marc Antony was secretly in love with her and wanted to help restore her family's empire across North Africa. As the two schemed together, mutterings spread through the Roman Senate that Cleopatra had too much power. Rome was scared that a powerful female pharaoh might inspire Roman women to rebel!

ROME COMES CALLING

By 30 BCE, Marc Antony had fled to Egypt to be with Cleopatra. Octavian, ruler of Rome, invaded Egypt to seize the royal lovers and bring them to Rome as his prisoners. Cleopatra was determined never to be captured, but Octavian's army was stronger and he had her swiftly arrested.

ON HER OWN TERMS

Bringing the queen of Egypt before him, Octavian taunted Cleopatra and threatened to take her to Rome in chains. In defiance, Cleopatra ordered her servants to sneak a basket of cobras to her room.

No-one knows what happened next, but it's widely believed that Cleopatra stuck her hand in the basket of poisonous snakes – receiving a fatal bite that caused her death – and denying Octavian his revenge. Cleopatra was the last of Egypt's great pharaohs.

Cleopatra came from a Greek family, but ruled Egypt as a pharaoh.

c. 61 CE
BOUDICA
THE QUEEN WHO DESTROYED ENTIRE CITIES

Deep in the mystical marshes of the east of England, lived one of the wealthiest tribes of ancient Britain. The Iceni were a proud people, led by a fierce queen: Boudica.

ROWDY ROMANS

Britain was invaded by the Roman Empire in 43 CE, and Boudica grew up in a divided homeland. The south was ruled by Rome, while the tribes of the north fought back against conquest. In the middle lay the lands of the Iceni.

Boudica's husband, King Prasutagus, wanted to be an ally of Rome. But when he died in 61 CE, the Romans invaded. They enslaved the Iceni, stole their lands, and subjected Boudica and her two daughters to brutal violence.

BOUDICA BITES BACK

Hell bent on revenge and determined to save her people, Boudica escaped. She jumped into a chariot with her daughters and called for all the tribes to join her in a mighty rebellion.

Boudica was an inspiring leader, able to quickly rally an army to march on Camulodunum. The Romans were terrified to see a woman leading such a large fighting force. Boudica's army tore down Camulodunum stone by stone, sometimes with their bare hands. They destroyed temples and houses, and drove the Romans away. It took them just two days to turn the whole city into rubble!

BURN IT ALL DOWN

Next they marched on the new Roman city of Londinium, and burned it to the ground. As the rest of the Romans fled, Boudica's army pushed on to Verulamium – destroying that too. The Roman Emperor Nero was so scared of Boudica, he wanted to end his invasion of Britain immediately.

UNKNOWN END

But, shortly after the battle of Verulamium, Boudica's rebellion was defeated. Her courageous stand was just not enough to match the military might of the well-trained Roman legions. The Romans went on to totally conquer Britain and Boudica disappeared. Some people even believe she is secretly buried under King's Cross Station in London.

DAMSELS BE DAMNED

ZENOBIA OF PALMYRA
c. 3rd Century

When her husband, King Odaenathus of Palmyra, was assassinated, the beautiful Queen Zenobia refused to give up her crown. She became a freedom fighter, determined to rescue her kingdom of Palmyra from the shackles of the Roman Empire. Leading a magnificent army, she conquered Syria, Egypt, and part of West Asia, and declared herself empress.

MATILDA OF TUSCANY
c. 1046–1115

Known as the Great Countess, Matilda was just a teenager when her father was murdered and her brother died in suspicious circumstances. Now the only heir to the powerful Margraviate (territory) of Tuscany, Matilda refused to follow the rules that demanded she hand over her family's lands to a male heir. Instead, she formed a powerful army and defended her rights and her castle.

ROYAL WOMEN WHO BESTED OTHERS IN BATTLE

TOMOE GOZEN 1157–1247

In Japan, women who became samurai fighters were known as onna-musha. Tomoe Gozen was a legendary onna-musha who commanded more than 800 samurai in battle. She carried a katana sword, traditionally a weapon only used by men, and was as bloodthirsty as she was terrifying – renowned for beheading all the generals she defeated!

AMINA OF ZAZZAU 1533–1610

As part of a royal family in what is now Nigeria, Amina was a powerful and respected princess. She was known for being a brave and courageous fighter who was a leading warrior in her brother's cavalry. Today, she is still celebrated in Hausa traditional songs as "Amina, daughter of Nikatau, a woman as capable as a man that was able to lead men to war."

Among the misty mountains of China, where the scent of cherry blossom filled the air, lived Princess Pingyang.

HUMBLE ORIGINS

Pingyang's father, Li Yuan, had been born poor, but rose to prominence as a great fighter. Before long, he was a general for Emperor Yangdi of the Sui dynasty – a cruel and heartless ruler. The emperor starved the poor and forced them to build grand canals and the Great Wall of China.

Many of the ordinary people rose up in rebellion against the emperor. They turned to Li Yuan, hoping he would help save them. But the emperor feared the growing power of his general and ordered the arrest and execution of Li Yuan.

LET THEM EAT!

Desperate to rescue her father, Pingyang opened up her family's great storehouses and fed all the people she could. She saved them from the emperor's famine, and in return, all the rural farmers and workers pledged their loyalty to Pingyang. They agreed to form an army to help rescue Li Yuan.

FIGHT LIKE A GIRL

Pingyang formed the "Army of the Lady", named for its unusual female leader. Women were not allowed to be fighters or generals, but in her determination she didn't care what anyone else thought.

The emperor's stuffy old generals weren't scared of an army of farmers led by a woman. But Pingyang's men were very well-behaved and soon she commanded more than 70,000 people. This epic force laid siege to the capital city, Chang'an, and dealt Emperor Yangdi and his armies a resounding defeat.

Pingyang's father, Li Yuan, was saved and became the new Chinese emperor – the first of the Tang dynasty. He bestowed the title of "princess" on his daughter in recognition of her role in fighting for his freedom.

DEATH WITH HONOUR

When the proud princess died, her father was devastated. He ordered that Pingyang should be given a military funeral, full of music and honour. This had never been allowed for a woman before. Many of his generals objected, but the new emperor demanded that his daughter would be shown the respect she had earned.

PINGYANG

c. 590–623

THE PRINCESS WHO RAISED AN ARMY TO SAVE HER FATHER

ÆTHELFLÆD

c. 870–918

THE QUEEN WHO DEFENDED HER HOME FROM THE VIKINGS

As the crackle of firewood filled the great dark hall, Æthelflæd, Lady of Mercia, readied her generals for battle. England was under attack. For 100 years, they had been fighting a dangerous enemy – the Vikings.

A NATION AT WAR

The Vikings were warriors from Denmark and Norway who piled into longships and crossed the rough seas to England. Up and down the coast they landed, raiding villages and towns – often burning them completely to the ground.

The kingdoms of England faced a tough battle against these unwelcome invaders. Æthelflæd's father, Alfred the Great, was King of Wessex – an area that covered much of southwest and southeast England – and had already fought long and hard to keep his territory.

Alfred loved his eldest daughter, Æthelflæd, very much. When she was just sixteen, Alfred decided Æthelflæd should marry King Æthelred, who ruled the neighbouring kingdom of Mercia.

A LEADING LADY

Æthelred was much older than Æthelflæd, and she soon took over running their kingdom so he could rest. She signed official documents and organized the protection of towns and villages from the Vikings. Her fame and power was just beginning.

> "SO POWERFUL THAT IN PRAISE AND EXALTATION OF HER WONDERFUL GIFTS, SOME CALL HER NOT ONLY LADY, BUT EVEN KING."
>
> HENRY OF HUNTINGDON, 12TH CENTURY

Æthelflæd not only showed everyone what a wise and gracious ruler she was, but people quickly learned she was also a brilliant military strategist. The noblemen of her kingdom soon united under her banner, and set off to fight the Vikings and drive them out of England once and for all!

VICTORY OVER THE VIKINGS

At the Battle of Tettenhall, Æthelflæd's army joined with her brother's Wessex forces to face the mighty Viking warlords Ingwaer, Eowils, and Halfdan. These three brothers ruled Northumberland and wanted Mercia for themselves.

Facing down the bloodthirsty Viking horde, Æthelflæd's men fought a dangerous and deadly battle. They were victorious, and all three Viking warlords were killed – severely weakening the Viking presence in England. Æthelflæd became known as a daring warrior queen.

FEARSOME FIGHTERS

Æthelflæd's armies didn't stop there. They continued to fight back against the Viking invaders. They rescued the city of Derby, then Leicester, and began to march on York. This was a major Viking stronghold, and the Vikings were so scared of Æthelflæd's army that they were ready to surrender before she even arrived!

TIME TO SHINE

Before the Norman Conquest of England in 1066, Anglo-Saxon women had a lot more rights in society than you might expect. Men and women were seen as pretty equal. Women were protected in law, could own houses and land, and were free to leave a marriage if it made them unhappy.

But the kingdom of Mercia was extra special. They believed that women had the right to rule. When King Æthelred died, the nobles of Mercia chose Æthelflæd as their queen. They didn't care that she wasn't a man; they just thought she was the best person for the job.

KEEP THE FAITH

Æthelflæd believed faith was just as important as war in defeating the Vikings. Christianity was a new religion, and Æthelflæd was the first to build many of the ancient churches that still exist in England today. She invested in monasteries, education, and the arts, making sure that Mercia became rich and prosperous. Her people were well taken care of, and no longer had to live in fear of being attacked by Viking raiders.

STOLEN LEGACY

By the time of her death, Æthelflæd was celebrated as one of the most important women of her time. She was buried at Gloucester, but was written out of history by chroniclers and later historians who dismissed her achievements and instead focused their attention on male figures.

They hid her away, but now history is fighting back! Recent research has placed Æthelflæd back in the narrative and revealed the impressive queen she really was.

A wyvern (two-legged dragon) was often associated with the kingdom of Wessex, while Mercia used a golden saltire (diagonal cross). Here they are shown merged together.

ARWA AL-SULAYHI
c. 1048–c. 1138

THE QUEEN WHO STOPPED AT NOTHING TO AVENGE HER FAMILY

As dry winds whipped sand around the mountains of Jabal Haraz, from their sides rose a terrifying fortress. A young queen surveyed her land from the tall turrets. She had only one thought on her mind: revenge.

RAISED TO RULE

An orphan since she was very young, Arwa had been raised in the court of Ali al-Sulayhi, the king of Yemen. Her family were part of the mountain peoples who had united all of Yemen after many bloody and deadly wars. A new religious group – Ismailism, a part of Shia Islam – bound the combined kingdom together. It brought strict beliefs on women's roles in society, barring them from holding any political or religious authority.

But Arwa's adopted family, although devoted believers, felt differently. King Ali passionately believed in his wife, Queen Asma, and her political insight. She was also a famous poet. King Ali saw her as an equal, and together they raised Arwa to know that a woman's place was not to be hidden away.

BRUTAL ATTACK

When Arwa was seventeen, she married King Ali's son, Al-Mukarram Ahmed. They had grown up happily together, and Al-Mukarram also believed that women could be powerful rulers. But as the young couple began their married life, tragedy struck their family.

As King Ali and Queen Asma set out on a pilgrimage to Mecca, their convoy was attacked by Sa'id Ibn Najah, an Ethiopian prince. King Ali was assassinated and Queen Asma taken prisoner. Sa'id Ibn Najah marched the widowed and weeping queen to a secret prison, and left her in a deep, cold cell, with no way of reaching her son. He even put the head of King Ali on a stake outside Queen Asma's prison cell – forcing her to look at it every day!

HOSTAGE HUNT

Al-Mukarram and Arwa searched high and low for his mother. But all they found were whispers and rumours of where she might be held. But then, after a year of silence, they finally learned the name of the secret place. →

Now king, Al-Mukarram set off on an arduous journey to rescue his mother and avenge his father. He took 3,000 furious soldiers who stormed the castle where she was being held, and Al-Mukarram himself descended into the vile dungeons to free her.

TRAGEDY STRIKES AGAIN

Although Al-Mukarram was successful, his struggle to free his mother left him traumatized. He returned to Arwa a shadow of his former self. With a husband to care for and their enemy Sa'id Ibn Najah still running free, Arwa took her court high into the mountains. From there, she began to plot her vengeance against the man who had stolen her mother-in-law, murdered her father-in-law, and deeply wounded her husband.

Since his terrible fight, King Al-Mukarram had been gravely ill. He knew he would never recover, and so ordered the kingdom to recognize that Arwa ruled in his name, and that all the power and the respect shown to him were to be shown to her as well.

PAYBACK TIME

Arwa was a clever and determined woman. As queen, she decided to spread rumours across her kingdom that her throne was weak and no-one wanted to support a woman ruling in the place of her husband. It wasn't long before these lies came to the ears of Sa'id Ibn Najah.

Deceived by Arwa's stories, he marched on her mountain fortress, prepared to win an easy victory and murder Arwa and Al-Mukarram to take the throne. Little did he know that the clever queen had played him for a fool! Her people had been lying in wait, and rose up against the invading army.

VICTORY LAP

Soon, the fight was over and Sa'id Ibn Najah's decapitated head was placed at Arwa's feet. Arwa marched at the head of her army, and proclaimed that a khutbah (a religious sermon) should be said in her name, alongside those for her husband, in the mosques across the country. This was the first time such an important religious speech had been given in a woman's name in Yemen. When Al-Mukarram died, Arwa went on to rule in her own right, without any male authority watching over her.

HONOURED AFTER DEATH

Arwa was seen as such a brilliant and courageous leader that she was even given the title of "Hujjah", which in Shia Islamic tradition raised her to the highest rank of religious authority in her country, second only to the Imam in Cairo. No Muslim woman had ever been granted such an honour before. She lived to the grand age of ninety – a wilful, determined queen, who fought back in times of trouble.

The Queen Arwa Mosque in Jiblah, Yemen was constructed by Arwa and she was later buried there.

Locked away in a castle in the middle of a deadly winter sat England's true heir – the Empress Matilda. For many years, her homeland had been stuck in a vicious war called the Anarchy, and now she was on the losing side.

BOLD BLOODLINE

Matilda was the granddaughter of William the Conqueror, the first Norman king of England, who had won the throne at the gruesome Battle of Hastings in 1066. Married off as a child to Henry V, the Holy Roman Emperor, she was crowned Empress Matilda when just a teenager. She soon proved herself to be a bold, reckless adventurer, marching over the Alps at Henry's side to confront the Pope, and even ruling Italy.

END OF AN EMPRESS

When Matilda was just twenty-three, Henry sadly died. There were few options for an empress without an emperor, and Matilda was given two choices for where her life would go.

She could become a nun, or marry someone else. So, a few years later, Matilda chose to marry Geoffrey, heir to the French Duchy of Anjou, and together they had three sons.

BACK ON HOME TURF
Matilda spent much of her time in England, because she was her father's only legitimate, surviving heir. But many of the barons didn't want to see a woman inherit the English throne, and when the king died, they rebelled against Matilda. They proclaimed that her cousin, Stephen, was the rightful heir, in part because he was a man!

STAKING HER CLAIM
Matilda refused to accept such an insult. She found her own allies and a vicious and deadly war was fought for many years. There was no clear winner until Stephen's forces managed to corner Matilda in Oxford Castle. Stephen thought she would surrender, but under the cover of darkness, and in a wild snowstorm, Matilda dressed herself in a white cloak and snuck over the ramparts of the castle. She crept past all the sleeping soldiers, and ran away to freedom!

Stephen was livid when he learned that she had escaped. But although he was crowned King of England soon after, Matilda had the last laugh. Stephen had to choose her eldest son, Henry, as his own heir, and so she made sure her bloodline would sit on the throne of England in the end.

7 FEBRUARY 1102 – 10 SEPTEMBER 1167
MATILDA
THE WOMAN WHO WOULDN'T TAKE "NO" FOR AN ANSWER

SUCCESSION SHAKERS

LIVIA DRUSILLA
59 BCE–29 CE

History has not been kind to Livia Drusilla – one of the most powerful women in ancient Rome, who was even given the title "Diva Augusta". The wife of Emperor Augustus, Livia was known for her power over him and her schemes to get her son on the throne. She is often remembered as intelligent and determined, but others claim she was sneaky, manipulative, and perhaps even a murderer!

WU ZETIAN
624–705

When the emperor of China died, Empress Wu refused to allow either of her sons to inherit the throne. She had been ruling in the emperor's place for many years, since he suffered a terrible illness, and she wasn't going to give up her power now. She even changed the name of the dynasty from Li (her husband's name) to Wu, and crowned herself emperor.

ROYAL WOMEN WHO TRIED TO TAKE THE THRONE

MARGARET OF ANJOU
1430–1482

Ruling at a time when the Christian Church thought women should never have any power, Margaret of Anjou was a force to be reckoned with. As her husband frequently struggled with his health, she often ruled alone as queen of England and France. Determined to protect her family at all costs, she got involved in the Wars of the Roses to try and destroy her enemies, but it destroyed her own family instead.

"PRINCESS" TARAKANOVA
1745–1775

Adventuress. Pretender. Fraud. There are a lot of things to be said about Princess Tarakanova. No-one knows who she really was, but she attempted to lay claim to the throne of the Russian empress, Catherine the Great, and raised an army to overthrow her. Arrested and imprisoned in St Petersburg, Tarakanova refused to reveal her real name, or where she was from.

ELEANOR OF AQUITAINE

c. 1124 – 1 April 1204

THE QUEEN WHO RULED TWO NATIONS

When Eleanor took the throne after her second marriage, she was on her way to becoming a legend. She was the first woman to be both queen of France and the queen of its mortal enemy – England.

SUBJECT OF SLANDER

Since her death, French chroniclers have attempted to erase Eleanor from history. They claimed that she was a murderer, had an affair with the Ottoman emperor, rode into battle bare-breasted, and seduced priests! Some of this gossip still survives today, but her real life was way more exciting.

Eleanor's father, the duke of Aquitaine, was one of the richest men in France. Her whole family were seen as scandalous because they traded with non-Christian cultures. But even though much of Europe disapproved of her family, Eleanor was still an incredibly rich heiress. Many attempts were made to kidnap her and force her to marry those who wanted her fortune!

TEEN QUEEN

When her father died, she found herself a ward of the king of France, Louis VI. He wanted to keep control of Eleanor's land and money, so he married her to his son. But then, to everyone's surprise, Louis died, and Eleanor became the teenage queen of France, along with her husband, Louis VII.

Unfortunately, the new King Louis was weak, jealous, and very annoying. He dragged Eleanor with him on a crusade – an attempt by Christian kings to seize the Holy Land in the Middle East.

TROUBLE IN PARADISE

After many problems along the way, they arrived in Antioch, which was governed by Eleanor's favourite uncle, Raymond of Poitiers. But, once there, Louis ignored everyone's advice and refused to help Raymond with his latest military campaign. Raymond quietly told his niece that she should divorce the French king.

This idea did not go down well with Louis. In a wild fit of rage, he accused Eleanor of having an affair with her uncle, and then carted her off to Tripoli, in North Africa, and placed her under house arrest.

PATIENT PRISONER

Eleanor was not at all impressed. Although divorce was almost unheard of at this time, she demanded one from Louis, and by the time they returned to Paris he agreed, thinking that Eleanor would have to spend the rest of her days as a nun in a convent.

Little did Louis know, Eleanor had already fallen in love with a dashing, handsome warrior – Prince Henry, Duke of Normandy, the son of Empress Matilda and heir to the English throne. Eleanor had to keep this secret, as England was France's mortal enemy, and as Duke of Normandy, Henry owed loyalty to the king of France. If he learned of their intentions, Louis could stop them marrying, and even execute Henry!

SECOND TIME LUCKY

At the very moment Louis and Eleanor's divorce was granted, she packed up her belongings, hot-footed it to Poitiers without a backwards glance, and immediately married Henry. Louis was absolutely outraged.

A year later, Henry became king of England. Unlike Louis, Henry quickly recognized that his wife was clever, witty, and a great politician. His lands now stretched from England and across central France, so he left his mother in charge of Normandy, and Eleanor ruled England when he was away.

Eleanor has been called the "grandmother of Europe" by historians, as so many of her children and grandchildren ruled countries and empires.

A LOVER SCORNED

But, distance creates discord, and soon word reached Eleanor that Henry had fallen in love with the beautiful Rosamund Clifford. She was devastated, and so hurt by Henry's betrayal that she left England and returned to her homeland of Aquitaine.

To add insult to injury, Henry refused to allow Eleanor to govern Aquitaine independently, even though the land had been hers before his. Angry at Henry's pigheadedness, Eleanor encouraged her four sons to rebel against their father. But Henry got wind of her plot and captured Eleanor on her way to Paris, imprisoning her for nearly sixteen years.

> "PITIFUL AND PITIED BY NO-ONE, WHY HAVE I COME TO THE IGNOMINY OF THIS DETESTABLE OLD AGE, WHO WAS RULER OF TWO KINGDOMS, MOTHER OF TWO KINGS?"
>
> **ELEANOR WRITING A LETTER TO THE POPE, 1193**

GRAND MATRIARCH

Eleanor was very, very bored. But her sons never gave up and eventually they defeated their father. Eleanor was set free and able to devote her energy towards helping them gain positions of influence. She lived well into her eighties, making sure her family became the powerful and legendary Plantagenet dynasty, which shaped English history for the next 300 years.

What would you do if your king betrayed you? This thought echoed through Joan of Flanders' mind as she read the latest news. Philip VI of France had lied to her and imprisoned her husband.

BRUTAL BETRAYAL

Having married the noble John de Montfort, Joan had lived a gentle life. Her husband had just been named heir to his half-brother's estate, the Duchy of Brittany, and their future life together seemed one of joy and hope.

But the dastardly French king had conspired to steal John's land and give it to his own nephew, Charles of Blois. He lured John to Paris – pretending to offer him safety – only to lock him up in prison and order an army to seize the duchy. He thought Joan was just a frightened, defenceless woman, and that his army would have no problem taking her lands.

> "THE COUNTESS OF MONTFORT WAS EQUAL TO A MAN FOR SHE HAD THE HEART OF A LION; AND, WITH A RUSTY SHARP SWORD IN HER HAND, SHE COMBATED BRAVELY."
>
> MEDIEVAL FRENCH CHRONICLER JEAN FROISSART

C. 1295 – SEPTEMBER 1374

JOAN OF FLANDERS

THE WOMAN WHO WENT INTO BATTLE TO GET HER HUSBAND BACK

FIGHTING BACK

Joan didn't like being threatened, and she definitely didn't like her husband being in jail. So she gathered her own army and moved to the fortified town of Hennebont. Here, she would make her stand. Philip's men soon arrived and attacked – putting the town under siege.

But Joan refused to be intimidated by her treacherous, lying opponent. The valiant countess jumped on the back of her great war horse, and picked up a sword. She rode from street to street, calling out to her people to join the fight. She even ordered all the women to help carry stones and pots of quicklime up to the ramparts of Hennebot's walls. They then threw these down on their attackers.

SUITING UP

Next, Joan put on a suit of armour, and charged out of Hennebot's gates with a brave battalion of 300 men. Roving across the battlefield as a fierce band, they set fire to the enemy's tents. As a leader, Joan was so terrifying that Philip's men nicknamed her "Jeanne la Flamme" (Joan the Flame). But her plans didn't stop there. For her next move, she led a pirate fleet to harass Philip's navy.

Joan was so dangerous that Philip eventually had to give in, and John was released. Thanks to her efforts, the lovers were united once more.

Imagine being betrothed to your future husband when you were just six years old! That is exactly what happened to Isabella d'Este, the original celebrity icon.

LAVISH LIFE

Granddaughter of the king of Naples and daughter of the duke of Ferrara, Isabella grew up with all the extravagance of an Italian court. Her world was full of velvet, gold, and jewels. Her dresses were made from the finest silks, and her education was the best that money could buy.

NOT JUST A PRETTY FACE

However, Isabella wasn't simply a preening, pampered princess. Her family were trailblazers in a new movement to give girls, as well as boys, a proper education. No longer were these aristocratic women just supposed to look pretty, get married to rich men, and have their babies. Isabella was raised to be smart, too – learning multiple languages and many other subjects.

LIFE AT COURT

When she was just fifteen, Isabella was sent to the court of her judgemental and weak husband, Francesco Gonzaga, Marquis of Mantua, but she rarely ever saw him. Instead, she was left to her own devices, roaming the great houses of Mantua and becoming a big supporter of the arts.

19 MAY 1474–13 FEBRUARY 1539
ISABELLA D'ESTE

THE SMART SOCIALITE WHO TOOK THE LEAD WHEN NEEDED

CULTURE VULTURE

Isabella loved music, fashion, art, and literature. She studied Latin, played the lute, and could discuss politics and philosophy better than most of the men who visited Mantua's court. She supported leading artists and thinkers, such as Michelangelo, Leonardo da Vinci, and Titian, and was renowned as a great collector of paintings, sculptures, and historical artefacts. If it was worth owning, Isabella had to have it.

SMARTS TO THE TEST

Collecting wasn't her only skill, and Isabella was clever, calm, and thoughtful. When Francesco was captured during a war in 1509, Isabella took over as ruler of Mantua. She fought for her husband's freedom and saved her city from a French invasion. But when Francesco was released, he was far from grateful. His people loved Isabella and thought she was a better ruler than he had ever been.

Embarrassed and humiliated, Francesco stripped Isabella of all her power. But when he died, Isabella became regent for their eldest son, and because of her, Mantua became a powerful city once more. A mere man would never be able to eradicate her legacy as one of the greatest figures of the Renaissance.

SCENE STEALERS

RANAVALONA I
1778–1861

For the people of Madagascar, Queen Ranavalona tried to be a mighty protector. Worried about colonization and the impact of visiting traders, Ranavalona thought she could defend her culture from the influences of Europe. She outlawed Christianity, drove out foreigners from her lands, and refused to trade with Europeans.

MYEONGSEONG
1851–1895

Known as Queen Min, Empress Myeongseong was determined to fight off both China and Japan's attempted invasion of Korea. She pushed for her country to become more modern, while championing Korean independence. She was assassinated by Japanese agents in 1895, but her death sparked major political change.

ROYAL WOMEN WHO WORKED TO SHAPE THE WORLD

SOPHIA DULEEP SINGH
1876–1948

Princess Sophia was determined to bring about change. Daughter of the last Sikh maharaja, Duleep Singh, Sophia grew up in England in the court of Queen Victoria. A suffragette, and a passionate believer in the rights of women, she braved abuse to stand on street corners and sell the idea of "Votes for Women" – dedicating her life to the task.

DIANA
1961–1997

Through her gentle charm and steely determination, Diana, "The People's Princess", won hearts across the world. Although her marriage to King Charles III of the United Kingdom was an unhappy one, Diana used her title and power to fight for those in need. She supported people with the illness AIDS and risked her own life to promote the campaign against landmines.

As salt filled the air, Sayyida al-Hurra watched as her fleet of pirate ships sailed out to sea. She was one of the most feared pirate queens to ever live, and all of the Mediterranean quivered at the sound of her name.

CAST OUT

From her base in the Moroccan town of Tétouan, Sayyida al-Hurra ruled without question. She had grown up as the child of refugees. Her parents were Sunni Muslims who left Granada in 1492, when all Spain's Muslims and Jews were persecuted and forced to leave, just because of their religions.

Her family had fled to Chefchaouen, the famous blue-painted city in Morocco, just before Sayyida al-Hurra was born. She had grown up to hate the Portuguese and Spanish invaders who drove her family away from their home.

LOCAL LEADER

At a young age, she had married the governor of Tétouan. She was often called on by him to solve problems, and ruled the city when he was away. When he died, the people of Tétouan accepted Sayyida al-Hurra as their leader and named her "al-Hurra", The Free Lady, to show that no man had power over her. →

C. 1485–1561
SAYYIDA AL-HURRA
THE PIRATE QUEEN WHO RULED THE SEAS

During her solo rule, her power and skills grew as she developed new ways to protect her town. Realizing the importance of having control over the seas, she expanded her fleet of ships – preparing for an era of piracy.

BRAVE BUCCANEER

Sayyida al-Hurra became one of the most formidable leaders of the corsairs of north Africa. She allied herself with the fearsome Ottoman pirates, the Barbarossa brothers. They ruled the sea to the east, and she controlled the west. The brothers transported Muslim and Jewish refugees who had been cast out of Spain, while she raided Christian ships to fund their campaign.

Her ships soon became well known in the Mediterranean. But Sayyida al-Hurra's seafaring exploits weren't just an act of revenge on the country that expelled her family. They were also part of a calculated strategy to defend her territory from the Europeans and gain money by making them buy back prisoners she'd taken.

ATTRACTIVE ALLY

Sayyida al-Hurra grew so powerful and so well respected that the sultan of Morocco, Ahmed al-Wattasi, begged her to marry him. She agreed on one condition: he would have to leave Fez, Morocco's capital city, and come to marry her in Tétouan.

No Moroccan monarch had ever married outside of Fez before. But the sultan was so eager to marry the pirate queen, and make her his ally, that he agreed. Their marriage made Sayyida al-Hurra queen of Morocco, but she kept her independence – staying in Tétouan to govern her mighty pirate fleet.

UNFAIRLY OUSTED

Sadly, her proud and happy rule could not last forever. Despite thirty years of steady leadership, her son-in-law, Muhammad al-Hassan al-Mandri, began to plot against her. He convinced the greedy nobles around her to overthrow The Free Lady and strip her of her power. Sayyida al-Hurra was banished to Chefchaouen, never to rule over her fleet again.

A LEGACY COMES TO LIGHT

The men of her own time, and those historians who came after her, viewed The Free Lady's story as too dangerous to retell. To them, a powerful pirate queen had no place in history, but now her story is beginning to be told once more.

Sayidda al-Hurra commanded an impressive fleet of ships that dominated the Mediterranean.

5 OCTOBER 1524 – 24 JUNE 1564
THE RANI DURGAVATI

THE TIGER HUNTER WHO RODE AN ELEPHANT INTO BATTLE

Queen and goddess, the Rani Durgavati was a fierce and impressive leader. This warrior queen loved her people, and even sacrificed her life to try and keep them safe.

UNSUITABLE SUITOR

The Rani was a Rajput princess, who grew up in the northern part of present-day India. By the time she was eighteen she had a reputation as an excellent horse rider, a celebrated beauty, and a skilled shot with a bow and arrow. She was so beloved by her father that he even allowed her to choose her own husband, a privilege denied to most young women at this time. But there was just one catch. Her husband had to be from a list of guests that her father had picked, and chosen on one specific night.

Unfortunately, the Rani had already fallen in love with a very handsome, but very unsuitable young man – Dalpat Shah, the eldest son of the king of Garha. The lovers had met in secret at local temples, and deep in the jungle during the wild hunts of their courts.

RUNAWAY BRIDE

The Rani's father refused to accept a son-in-law who was a Gond (from the kingdom of Garha). So the young couple decided they had no choice but to call on the ancient tradition of "harana vivah", where a bride invites her champion to fight for her hand.

Madly in love, Dalpat Shah mustered forces of more than 12,000 men, and marched upon the army of the Rani's father, defeating him in battle. Then he carried away his bride-to-be to his well-fortified mountain castle, Singorgarh Fort, and after a lavish twelve-day-long wedding, made her his queen.

TIGER HUNTER

But danger stalked the land of Garha. Fierce tigers crept out of the jungle and stole babies in the night, snatched workers from their fields, and ate weary travellers who were not safely in their homes by nightfall. The Rani took it upon herself to hunt down these creatures to protect her people.

One day, on a tiger hunt, the Rani chose to ride her new elephant, Sarman. Suddenly, the tiger she was hunting sprang out of the undergrowth and attacked them. Sarman was badly wounded, but despite his injuries, he did not flee the scene – keeping the Rani safely on his back until she had killed the dangerous beast.

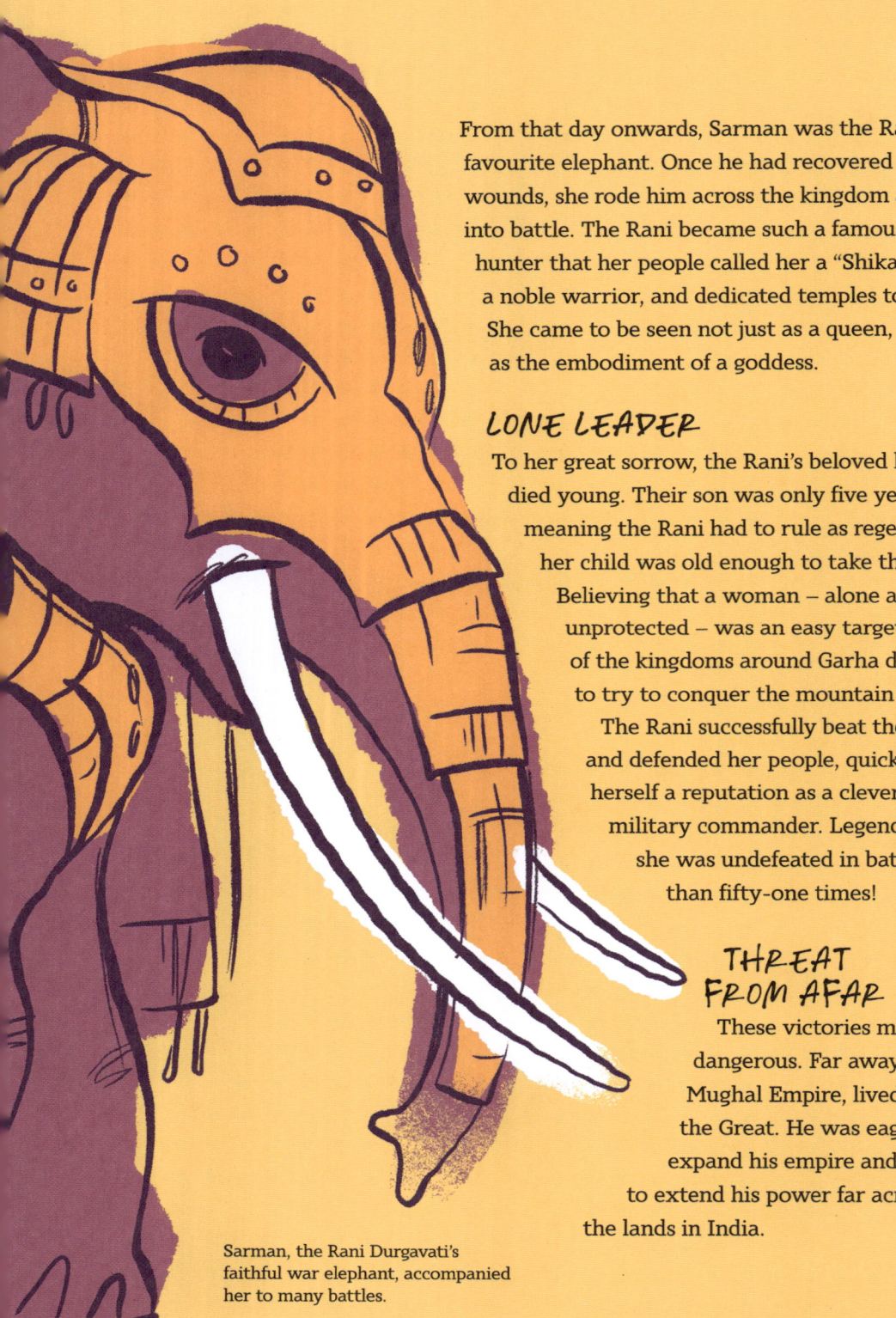

From that day onwards, Sarman was the Rani's favourite elephant. Once he had recovered from his wounds, she rode him across the kingdom and even into battle. The Rani became such a famous tiger hunter that her people called her a "Shikari", a noble warrior, and dedicated temples to her. She came to be seen not just as a queen, but as the embodiment of a goddess.

LONE LEADER

To her great sorrow, the Rani's beloved husband died young. Their son was only five years old, meaning the Rani had to rule as regent until her child was old enough to take the throne. Believing that a woman – alone and unprotected – was an easy target, many of the kingdoms around Garha decided to try to conquer the mountain country. The Rani successfully beat them all back and defended her people, quickly earning herself a reputation as a clever and fearless military commander. Legend has it that she was undefeated in battle more than fifty-one times!

THREAT FROM AFAR

These victories made her dangerous. Far away in the Mughal Empire, lived Akbar the Great. He was eager to expand his empire and wanted to extend his power far across the lands in India.

Sarman, the Rani Durgavati's faithful war elephant, accompanied her to many battles.

Akbar heard rumours of a powerful, dangerous Indian queen and decided that her lands must belong to him. First, he sent the Rani a golden spinning wheel to remind her that, as a woman, her place was at home, not on the battlefield. Then he sent 10,000 of his fiercest warriors across the mountains to try and capture Garha.

THE RECKONING

Akbar's army was led by a strong general, Asaf Khan. Hearing the march of battle drums, the Rani moved her base of operations to Chauragarh Fort, nestled deep in the mountains. She raised an army of 20,000 soldiers and 700 elephants, even setting up a powerful battalion of female warriors who answered directly to her.

Then the fateful day of battle arrived. Asaf Khan's men came to the valley of Narrai, and the Rani rode out to meet them in battle on Sarman. Three times the Rani managed to push the Mughal army back, but her enemy had brought a weapon she never expected to face.

DEADLY DEFEAT

Asaf Khan filled the valley with cannon fire and killed many of the Rani's brave defenders. The days of fighting wore on, until finally only 300 men remained with her, and they were hopelessly outnumbered. As the Mughal attackers rained down cannonballs and arrows, the Rani suffered two terrible wounds – taking arrows to both her face and to her neck. She fainted, falling from the safety of Sarman's back directly onto the battlefield.

A WARRIOR'S END

As the Rani came to, she looked at the devastation around her. Sarman had fallen to his knees, full of arrows. Without the safety of her brave battle elephant, the Rani knew that the fight was lost. She stayed close to Sarman and chose to die next to him.

Even after her death, the Rani was still adored by her people. She was buried with two rocks by her side, to symbolize the drums she had beaten to call everyone to battle. Some villages still swear they can hear the drums beating, calling the Rani's followers to battle for eternity.

Taking the throne at a time of turmoil, Elizabeth I knew it wouldn't be long before advisors were pestering her to get married. But, throughout her reign, she said "no!" – staying a single lady until the very end.

UNWANTED HEIR

Elizabeth had a rocky start in life. When she was just two years old, her father, Henry VIII of England, executed her mother, Anne Boleyn. Then, he declared Elizabeth was illegitimate, and out of the line of succession. He didn't want a mere daughter to inherit his throne.

Not only was this very cruel – not to mention rude – but Elizabeth and her older half-sister, Mary, had to put up with their father marrying four other women and beheading one more of them, before he died in 1547.

FRACTURED NATION

Henry VIII had torn his country apart. He changed England's religion from Catholicism to a new religion he set up – English Protestantism – partly so that he could divorce his first wife, and marry Elizabeth's mother, Anne. Many of the noble families liked the idea of religious changes and an English church, but others were upset by the move. Differences in religion set neighbour against neighbour, putting the country on the brink of civil war.

Before Henry VIII died, he wanted to make sure that his country stayed Protestant, and so he demanded that his young son, Edward, make sure that his older sister, Mary, who was Catholic, could never inherit the throne.

7 SEPTEMBER 1533 – 24 MARCH 1603
ELIZABETH I
THE QUEEN WHO WOULD NOT WED

FAMILY FEUD

But when Edward was tragically killed by a terrible illness, trouble began. Mary's supporters rallied to the flag of the Catholic princess. They executed Lady Jane Grey, who Edward had named as his successor, and instead installed Mary as the new monarch.

Throughout all of this, Elizabeth watched and waited. But now that her sister was on the throne, her life was in danger. Mary knew that the new Protestants would rally behind Elizabeth and put the Protestant princess on the throne if they could.

Believing that Elizabeth would lead a mighty rebellion against her, Mary imprisoned her little sister inside the dank dungeons of the Tower of London. Then she set about on her campaign to make England Catholic again, even marrying Philip II of Spain – another Catholic monarch – and hoping to produce an heir to come before Elizabeth in the succession. But their marriage was deeply unhappy. Within two years Mary was dead and England had yet another new monarch.

GOOD QUEEN BESS

Elizabeth was just twenty-five, but now she was queen of a wounded country and a people traumatized by her family's actions. She wanted to fix the nation's problems. Personally, Elizabeth was a big believer in astrology. John Dee, a magician who claimed to speak to angels, was one of her most treasured advisors, and she would often turn to him for advice about the stars.

PEER PRESSURE

Although her rule was popular, many of the men around her began to pressure Elizabeth into making a strong political marriage. But as a queen, this was no easy task. Few men were her equal, and many of them wanted to use her power for themselves.

Elizabeth was often depicted wearing pearls – a symbol of wealth, purity, and her unwed status.

Not wanting to give up her authority, Elizabeth vowed that she would never, ever marry. "If I follow the inclination of my nature, it is this: beggar-woman and single, far rather than queen and married," she declared.

THREAT FROM THE SEA

Her biggest enemy was Spain. Still angry at losing the English throne after the death of his wife, Philip II of Spain was determined to take back the country at any cost. In 1588, he sent the Spanish Armada, a huge fleet of war ships, all the way to England in an attempt to conquer the country.

When Elizabeth heard what was sailing over the waves to greet her brave sailors, she rode out to meet her troops on the Essex coast. Wearing a silver breastplate over a velvet dress, her red hair piled high and laced with pearls, she addressed her "loving people", crying out:

> "I KNOW I HAVE THE BODY OF A WEAK AND FEEBLE WOMAN, BUT I HAVE THE HEART AND STOMACH OF A KING… AND THINK FOUL SCORN THAT… ANY… SHOULD DARE TO INVADE THE BORDERS OF MY REALM!"

SNEAK ATTACK

Elizabeth's navy was led by Sir Francis Drake, a well-known rapscallion and pirate. He decided the only way to defeat Spain was with a dangerous and cunning plan. He set fire to his own ships and sailed them into the Spanish fleet late at night. The closely packed ships fled from the fire, making them vulnerable to attack, and Philip's navy was defeated. Elizabeth's realm was defended and her reign secured.

NOT TYING THE KNOT

TOMYRIS OF THE MASSAGETAE   c.500

Ruler of the Massagetae in Asia, Queen Tomyris was a tough leader. After she rejected an offer of marriage from Cyrus the Great, King of Persia, he invaded her lands to take them by force. Tomyris destroyed Cyrus's army, and then beheaded the king – stuffing his head into a wine barrel full of blood in revenge!

BASINA AND CLOTILDA   c.590

These royal cousins were unstoppable. As the daughters of two French kings, Basina and Clotilda were ordered away from court after a number of family assassinations left them unprotected. Forced to live in a convent and become nuns, these princesses led a scandalous revolt against their wicked and cruel abbess.

ROYAL WOMEN WHO CHOSE TO STAY SINGLE

ST AGNES OF BOHEMIA
1211–1282

When the Holy Roman Emperor, Frederick II, saw this Bohemian princess, he fell madly in love. But Agnes didn't want to be his third wife, especially as she was already engaged to one of his sons. Frederick swore that if she married any other man, he'd take his revenge. Rejecting his cruel demands, Agnes chose to stay single and become a nun instead.

IRENE OF GREECE AND DENMARK
11 MAY 1942–

After World War I, the Greek people chose to get rid of their monarchy. Born in exile, Irene became a princess without a country. She has lived in India and Spain, is a brilliant musician, and to this day has refused to marry. Instead, she chooses to keep her independence and devotes her life to making the world a better place.

As the carriage crashed, then rolled over, everyone screamed. But Christina laughed to herself. She had just abdicated the royal throne of Sweden, and was on the run, leaving her country before anyone could force her to come back.

Thrown from the carriage, her dress ended up over her head. As she pulled herself up, she loudly declared that now everyone would know she was "neither male nor hermaphrodite, as some people in the world have pass'd me for."

TURNING HEADS

There had long been rumours about Queen Christina. She just didn't behave like a woman was supposed to. When she was born, Christina was covered in hair all over her body, and had such a loud strong cry that the midwives thought she was a boy.

Although Gustav, King of Sweden, was happy to have a daughter, his wife, Maria Eleonora of Brandenburg, had longed for a son. Maria thought Christina was ugly, and she was often cruel and mean to her. But Gustav loved Christina deeply, and took her away with him on many trips.

WHAT A BLAST!

Gustav even took Christina on military engagements. Once, the commander of a heavily armed fortress was concerned that the noise of the guns might upset the baby princess and asked if they should stop firing. The king thought for a moment, and then replied, "Let them fire! She is the daughter of a soldier, and it is proper that the sound should be familiar to her!"

Instead of being frightened by the loud explosions, Christina was delighted, laughing and clapping her hands with each massive bang. Gustav offered to take Christina with him into battle so she could learn to fight, but before he could fulfil his promise, he died. Christina was only six.

NOT LIKE OTHER GIRLS

As heir to the throne, Christina was given the best tutors, and an education that was unrivalled in politics and the sciences. From childhood, she learned eleven languages, along with ancient history, literature, and art. But being so educated made her very different to all the other women in the Swedish court, and she found them really boring and annoying.

Her disdain worsened when her mother suddenly ran away, abandoning Christina to be brought up by the powerful men around her. She began to despise the way women behaved, with their lack of education and their fascination with needlework and babies.

18 DECEMBER 1626 – 19 APRIL 1689
CHRISTINA OF SWEDEN
THE WOMAN WHO DRESSED LIKE A MAN

Christina greeted the Pope wearing a hat with a huge plume of white feathers.

"For a woman to acquit herself with dignity in the duties of a throne," Christina wrote of the ladies around her, "… is almost an impossibility. The ignorance of women, their imbecility of soul, body, and understanding, render them incapable of government." Pretty harsh stuff.

REASONABLE REIGN

At eighteen, Christina was crowned and began to rule. She became an international diplomat, helping to end the Thirty Years War in Europe. She also enjoyed collecting artworks and books, met famous philosophers such as René Descartes, and wanted to add an Academy of Sciences to Sweden to improve everyone's education.

> "IT IS IMPOSSIBLE FOR ME TO MARRY. I AM ABSOLUTELY CERTAIN ABOUT IT. I DO NOT INTEND TO GIVE YOU REASONS. MY CHARACTER IS SIMPLY NOT SUITED TO MARRIAGE."
>
> CHRISTINA, WRITING IN 1649

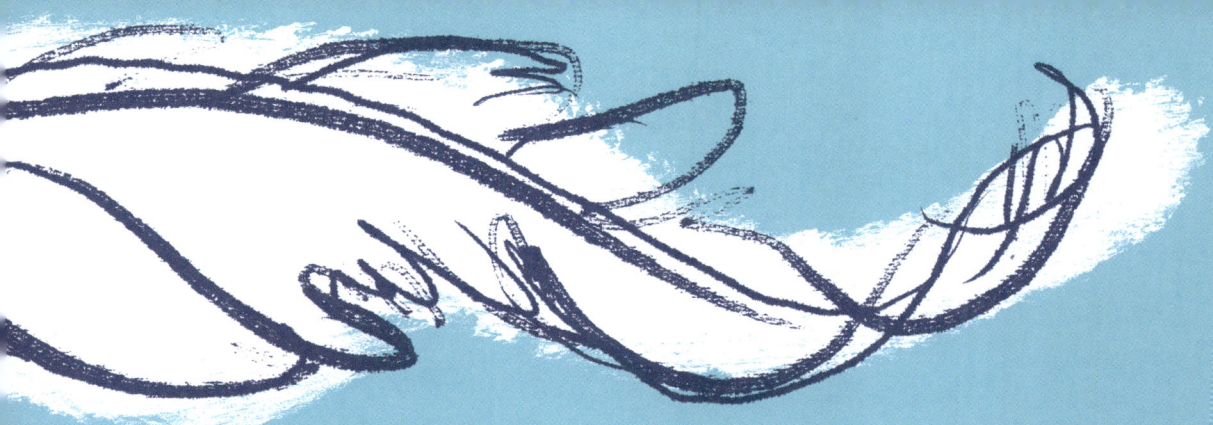

But although the young queen was widely adored, she was desperately unhappy. Christina longed for a private life and to be free. She hated the monotony of the duties of state. She was bored, and resented the expectation that she would have to marry and continue the family dynasty.

ENOUGH IS ENOUGH

Christina had also fallen in love with a woman – her lady-in-waiting, Ebba Sparre, who she was known to share a bed with. With no plans to marry and feeling fed up, after ten years Christina decided to abdicate. "I have absolutely resolved to retire," she told her people. She left Sweden under cover of night, and began a metamorphosis.

PLAYING WITH GENDER

"Now I will be a man!" Christina joyfully declared. Casting off female clothing and putting on the garb of a young nobleman, Christina took the title of Count de Dohna. Next, she dismissed all of her ladies-in-waiting, and travelled with only three young noblemen.

"She had not the least resemblance of a woman," wrote a confused French ambassador. He also criticized her modesty, saying she was waited on by men at all hours, and chose to take a masculine appearance.

LIVING IT UP

Christina spent her time travelling around Europe, enjoying her liberty. When she visited Rome, the Pope put on a huge welcome, and Christina rode in dressed in men's clothing, with an especially flamboyant hat. Throughout her life, she choose to dress in the clothes of both men and women and spent her time as a patron of the arts. "I was not born to be the slave of custom!" she proudly declared.

CATHERINE I
1684–1727
THE PEASANT WHO BECAME A QUEEN

Raised far away from palaces, through a stroke of fortune Catherine I went on to become one of the first in a line of formidable female rulers of Russia.

ORPHAN GIRL

No-one knows the true story of Catherine's birth. Some people claim her father was a grave digger, others that he was a farmer from Belarus, and that her mother was a poor woman from Latvia. Whatever the real story, in 1689, when Catherine was just a child, plague came to her village and killed her parents.

An unkind widow adopted her, keeping Catherine as a scullery maid and forcing her to do the laundry in their house – like a real life Cinderella! The widow refused to let Catherine learn to read or write and treated her appallingly.

ROUGH TREATMENT

As Catherine grew into a beautiful young woman, her cruel caretaker became jealous, and suspicious that her son or her husband might fall in love with the poor orphan. She conspired to marry Catherine off to a Swedish dragoon, a military officer, when she was just seventeen.

This hasty marriage lasted all of eight days, until Russian forces invaded Latvia and Catherine's husband ran away with his regiment. Catherine was left behind without anyone to protect her.

PRETTY PRIVILEGE

But Catherine's beauty stopped the invading soldiers in their tracks, and they quickly decided to take her back to Russia with them. Captivated by her looks, Peter the Great, Russia's tsar, invited Catherine to live with him in Saint Petersburg.

Here, in a tiny log cabin, he secretly married the orphaned laundry maid. Catherine was so important to Peter that he refused to travel anywhere without her, even taking her with him on dangerous military campaigns.

SEALING THE DEAL

Peter and Catherine were a happy couple, but to the wider world she was still just his mistress. When the Ottoman vizier, Mehmet Pasha, surrounded Peter and Catherine with his troops during the deadly Russo-Ottoman War, Catherine saved Peter's life by giving away all her jewellery in exchange for their safe passage back to Russia.

Although Peter was humiliated by the defeat, he was overjoyed by Catherine's cleverness. He decided to marry her officially and make her Empress of Russia, legitimizing all their children.

THE START OF A STORY

When Peter died, Catherine ruled alone. It was the first time a woman had ever governed Imperial Russia, and she was its first queen to have been born in poverty. She only held the throne for two years until her death, but her fair governance paved the way for many other great women.

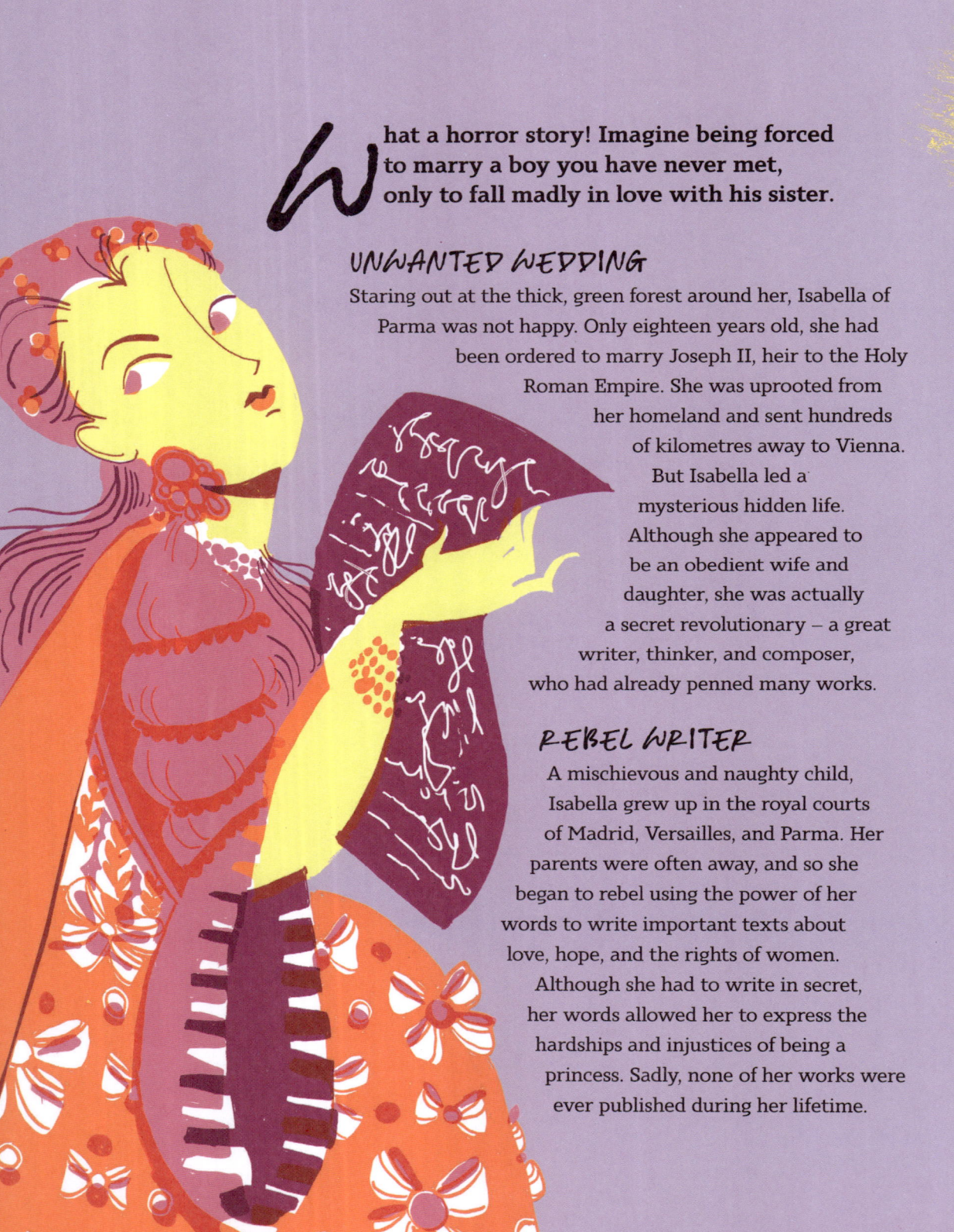

What a horror story! Imagine being forced to marry a boy you have never met, only to fall madly in love with his sister.

UNWANTED WEDDING

Staring out at the thick, green forest around her, Isabella of Parma was not happy. Only eighteen years old, she had been ordered to marry Joseph II, heir to the Holy Roman Empire. She was uprooted from her homeland and sent hundreds of kilometres away to Vienna. But Isabella led a mysterious hidden life. Although she appeared to be an obedient wife and daughter, she was actually a secret revolutionary – a great writer, thinker, and composer, who had already penned many works.

REBEL WRITER

A mischievous and naughty child, Isabella grew up in the royal courts of Madrid, Versailles, and Parma. Her parents were often away, and so she began to rebel using the power of her words to write important texts about love, hope, and the rights of women. Although she had to write in secret, her words allowed her to express the hardships and injustices of being a princess. Sadly, none of her works were ever published during her lifetime.

ISABELLA OF PARMA
31 December 1741 – 27 November 1763
The great writer who lived in secret

The Fate of a Princess
Devastated by the unexpected death of her mother from smallpox just weeks before her eighteenth birthday, Isabella became deeply melancholy and convinced that she would also die young. Her mother's final wish had been that Isabella would marry Joseph II, and this she had dutifully done.

But not long after she arrived in Vienna, something unexpected happened. Isabella fell passionately in love with Joseph's sister, Marie Christina. The two became inseparable and Isabella sent her more than 200 letters that still survive today. "I live to love you," she wrote. "My happiness is to love you and to be loved by you."

> "What should the daughter of a great prince expect? Her fate is, without doubt, most unhappy. She is from birth the slave of people's prejudices."
>
> **— Isabella, in her work "The Fate of Princesses"**

Unhappy End
Despite her new love, Isabella remained overwhelmed by an inescapable sadness, worried her prophecy of an early death would come true. And, to everyone's shock, it did. Isabella died of smallpox when she was only twenty-one, just as she had foretold – cutting her brilliant life short.

LEADING LADIES

ISABELLA OF CASTILE 1451–1504

When Isabella married Ferdinand II of Aragon, she agreed to unite their lands, Castile and Aragon, for the first time. Together, they created the Spanish Empire. But although Isabella was intelligent and resourceful, she could also be very cruel. In 1492, she forced all the Jews and Muslims living in Spain to leave, just because they were a different religion to her.

ANNE OF DENMARK 1574–1619

Often overlooked while her husband, James I, united England and Scotland and hunted for witches, Anne was a bold and surprising woman. While James could be moody and unkind, Anne refused to ever let him bully her. She fought for the right to see her children, demanded to have rebellious and radical ladies-in-waiting, and became a dedicated supporter of the arts.

ROYAL WOMEN WHO STOLE THE SPOTLIGHT

CHARLOTTE OF BELGIUM 1840–1927

Married to an Austrian archduke, Princess Charlotte soon found herself sent across the seas with her husband to be crowned Empress of Mexico. She became famous for her diplomacy and determination. When Mexico's civil war broke out, Charlotte sailed to Europe to plead for aid. She headed to the centre of the Catholic Church, the Vatican, and staged a sit-in – refusing to leave until help was promised.

ZEWDITU OF ETHIOPIA 1876–1930

Born to one of Emperor Menelik II's consorts, Zewditu caused trouble from the moment she was born. When Queen Bafena heard of Zewditu's birth, she took up arms against the emperor to punish him. But little did she know this tiny baby girl would go on to be the first and only woman to rule Ethiopia in her own right. Zewditu dedicated her life to promoting unity across her country, and all of Africa.

24 MAY 1819 – 22 JANUARY 1901
VICTORIA
THE QUEEN WHO KNEW HER OWN MIND

Within the grand surroundings of Westminster Abbey, a teenage Victoria bent to receive the crown. But, little known to onlookers, Britain's new young queen wouldn't be just a political pawn – she would shape an entire era.

YOUNG AND FREE

Victoria came to the throne when she was just eighteen years old, but the young queen refused to get married straight away. Her childhood had been strict – with her every move controlled by her mother – so now was her time to take back her freedom and use her own judgement.

She wanted to have fun, and fell in love with many of the young princes who visited her court. Alexander Nikoláyevich, heir to the Russian Empire, really caught her eye, but Victoria knew she would never give up her throne to marry him and move to Russia.

GOSSIP GIRL

Victoria also loved to gossip. When she was just twenty years old, she shocked everyone by starting a vicious rumour about one of her ladies-in-waiting, Lady Flora Hastings – claiming that she was having a baby with a married man! She insisted Flora had an examination to prove she wasn't pregnant or else she'd be banned from court.

But Victoria soon learned that mean girl behaviour comes with some nasty consequences. Lady Flora Hastings died from a fatal disease and everyone discovered that there wasn't any truth in the rumours Victoria had been spreading about her.

KEEPING FRIENDS CLOSE

Despite her error, Victoria still didn't want to play by the rules of the time. When a new government was elected by the British people, she refused to allow any of their wives to become her ladies-in-waiting. Instead, she wanted to keep the women she already had. Many of these were the wives and relatives of ministers from the opposing party, but to Victoria they were her friends.

Victoria's actions weren't just a social snub. They showed she wouldn't listen to her new ministers, or allow them any influence in her household, and so they were unable to form a government. This triggered a major crisis, and the British people were very angry.

BEAT THAT!

Victoria lived a long life, marrying Prince Albert of Saxe-Coburg and Gotha and giving birth to nine children. But she continued to flout conventions up until the end. After Albert died, she became close friends with her Scottish manservant John Brown, leading to outrage from her government and the press. They were terrified that Victoria and John might have secretly married! But Victoria didn't care what others thought, and kept John by her side.

Even though she faced much criticism and even attempts on her life, Victoria ended up reigning for almost sixty-four years. She is one of the United Kingdom's longest reigning monarchs.

Deep in the Forbidden City, behind the walls of the Zhongcui Palace, plotted the cunning and clever Empress Dowager Cixi. For fifty years she ruled China, and is even thought to have used poison to get her way!

EAGER TO IMPRESS

The Yehe Nara clan of Manchuria were noble warriors. As the daughter of a powerful duke, Cixi had a privileged childhood, and, at the age of sixteen, her father decided to offer her to the Chinese emperor as his wife. Cixi's father respected her clever mind and thought she would be a savvy political operator.

But becoming the emperor's wife was not a straightforward task. As Cixi arrived in the royal palace, she realized she was going to be just one of sixty other candidates, all young noblewomen, who were all fighting for a chance to marry Yizhu, the young Xianfeng Emperor.

PROXIMITY TO POWER

Although Cixi wasn't chosen as the emperor's wife, she did become a concubine (a mistress who still spent time with him), and lived with a large group of wives and concubines in the large palace known as the Forbidden City. She rose through the ranks and soon gave birth to the emperor's only son, Zaichun, in 1856.

29 NOVEMBER 1835 – 15 NOVEMBER 1908

CIXI

THE WOMAN WHO MAY HAVE POISONED HER WAY INTO POWER

FINDING FRIENDS

Inside the Forbidden City, while the other women plotted and tried to take revenge for the smallest insults, Cixi became close friends with the emperor's wife, the Empress Ci'an. As best friends, the two looked out for each other.

After the emperor's death in 1861, Cixi's five-year-old son became the Tongzhi Emperor. The previous emperor had selected eight powerful noblemen to act as regents until the boy was old enough to rule on his own. But Cixi and Ci'an formed an alliance, and conspired together to seize power and rule instead. The two friends imprisoned five of the regents, executed one, and even ordered the final two to carry out their own deaths!

GIRL POWER

Together they ruled as co-Empress Dowager, until Ci'an's death in 1881. From a low-level concubine to the leader of a nation, Cixi had ascended with determination, and she had grown used to the power of being empress. Even though her own son had died in 1875, she had managed to install her nephew, Guangxu, as the new emperor in his place. But people soon spread a rumour that she had poisoned her own son to keep control of the throne.

BEHIND THE SCENES

The new emperor was just a puppet king. In reality, it was still Cixi who ruled the Chinese Empire from the shadows. Even though she was barred from sections of the Forbidden City, where only the emperor was allowed to go, Cixi selected trusted men to work for her, carrying out her wishes and removing anyone who got in her way.

But in 1898, the young emperor was found to be plotting Cixi's assassination. In revenge, she had him placed under house arrest, removing him from power and finally making clear that she was the one in charge of China.

POISON PLOT?

In 1908, Emperor Guangxu suddenly died of arsenic poisoning. To everyone's shock, Cixi died the next day, and many historians have wondered if it was a double arsenic murder plot gone wrong. Did Cixi poison Guangxu, or did Guangxu poison Cixi?

No-one will ever know for sure. Later historians have viewed Cixi in different ways – seeing her as both a ruthless ruler and steadfast governor who was keen to do her best for the country. But, above all, her legacy as a clever conspirator who clung to power lives on to this day.

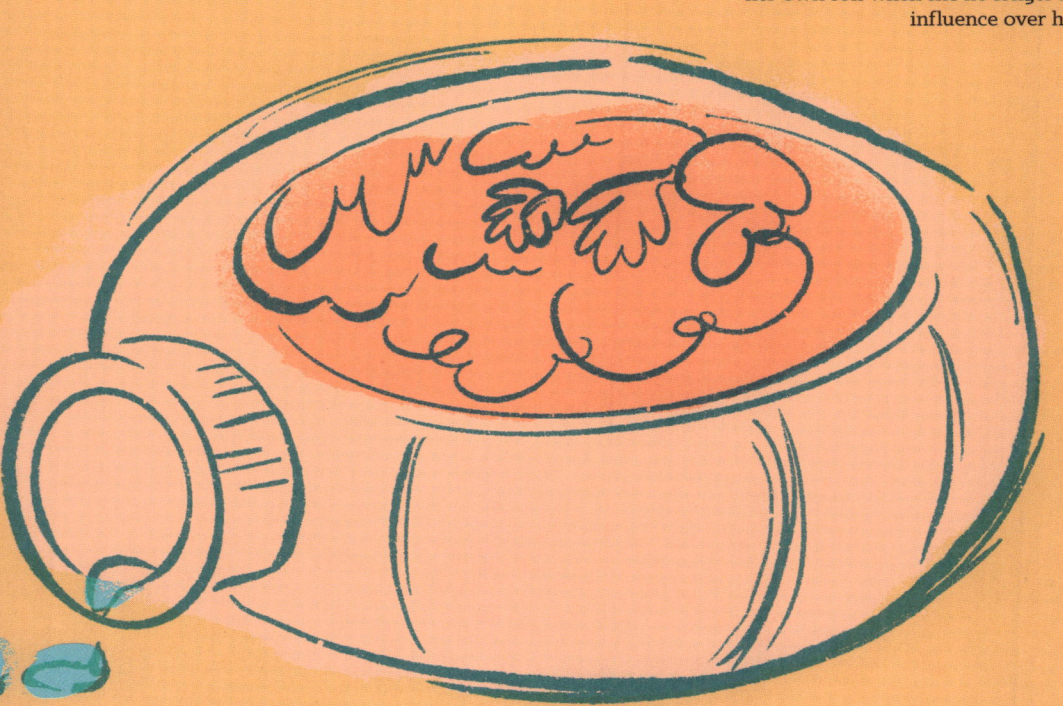

Cixi was rumoured to have poisoned her own son when she no longer had influence over him.

A respected Queen Mother, Yaa Asantewaa spent her time cultivating crops until a sudden war rocketed her to the centre of a rebellion.

MOTHER TO ALL

Back in the 19th century, the Asante Empire lay at the heart of present-day Ghana. It encompassed many different small kingdoms, including the powerful land of Ejisu, home to Yaa Asantewaa. She lived peacefully as a farmer while her brother, Nana Akwasi Afrane Okese, was a powerful and respected ruler. He appointed Yaa Asantewaa as Queen Mother of the Ejisu – a highly important advisory role that gave her power and respect.

Her main duty was to be the protector of the Golden Stool – the sacred symbol and throne of her people. The Asante believed that the stool held all the souls in their kingdom – living, dead, and those yet to be born.

UNRULY INVADERS

But this was a dangerous time. Europeans had arrived many centuries earlier, and were stripping the African Gold Coast of its people, culture, and land. For a long time, the Asante had been at war with European powers, but things were about to get much worse.

In 1896, the British invaded, exiling the king and the government of Asante. Then they demanded that Yaa Asantewaa hand over the Golden Stool.

→

YAA ASANTEWAA
c. 1840 – 17 OCTOBER 1921
THE WOMAN WHO WENT FROM FARMER TO FIGHTER

For four long years, she kept it safe and hidden as the British hunted for it. They didn't realize that Yaa Asantewaa was dangerous, and no longer just a peaceful farmer. She now saw herself as the protector of her people and was not going to hand over their souls to any man!

GREED FOR GOLD

As war raged, the gall of the invaders grew. The leader of the British troops, Governor Frederick Hodgson, gravely insulted the Asante people when he reached the capital of Kumasi. "Where is the Golden Stool?" he demanded. "I am the representative of the Paramount Power. Why have you relegated me to this ordinary chair?" He demanded they hand over their precious artefact. Such rude words demanded a response.

In secret, Yaa Asantewaa brought together all the remaining rulers of the Asante, and together they planned their revenge. She saw that some of the leaders were reluctant to fight and gave an epic war speech, saying:

> "I MUST SAY THIS, IF YOU, THE MEN OF ASANTE, WILL NOT GO FORWARD, THEN WE WILL. WE, THE WOMEN, WILL. I SHALL CALL UPON MY FELLOW WOMEN. WE WILL FIGHT! WE WILL FIGHT TILL THE LAST OF US FALLS IN THE BATTLEFIELDS."

LET'S SHOW THEM!

This was a call to arms, to revolution, to drive the British out of her land. The chiefs were ashamed of their cowardice and named Yaa Asantewaa "Sahene" (war-leader) for her fearless bravery. It was the first time an Asante woman had ever been given this honour.

Soon, all the Asante knew that Yaa Asantewaa was leading an army against the British troops. Clad proudly in batakarikese – ceremonial battle dress – she rallied thousands to her call. Then they began a deadly attack.

Although the Asante were able to drive the British back towards the coast, their enemy had brought a dangerous new technology – the Maxim machine gun. Thousands of Yaa Asantewaa's soldiers were brutally slaughtered by British bullets and she was captured and exiled to the Seychelles.

SECRET KEEPER

Yaa Asantewaa was joined in exile by the king of the Asante, Prempeh I. For the rest of her life, she was not allowed to return home. But all was not lost. In those twenty years, Yaa Asantewaa made sure the British never found the Golden Stool.

When King Prempeh I's exile ended, he returned to Ghana, and his people. Ruler once more, he proudly brought back the bones of Yaa Asantewaa, to be buried in her homeland. Today, her defiance, her bravery, and her belief in the power of women are still proudly honoured in Ghana.

The Golden Stool lay hidden in secret for decades, until it was rediscovered in 1921.

YAA ASANTEWAA

13 MARCH 1900 – 16 DECEMBER 1965
SĀLOTE TUPOU III
THE QUEEN WHO SURVIVED DEATH TWICE

Although she became the longest reigning Tongan monarch in history, as a child Queen Sālote Tupou III nearly lost her chance to rule.

PROUD ISLAND

When people first arrived on the island of Tonga 3,000 years ago, they had little knowledge that one day they would be ruled by a tough and memorable queen. Her name was Sālote Tupou III. Her people were Pacific Islanders, and had once ruled over a proud empire of land and sea. But in the year Sālote Tupou was born, they had become part of the British Empire.

Her parents had loved each other very much, and Sālote was their only child. But their marriage had caused much upset among their people, as Queen Lavinia was not seen as a noble wife for the king.

CHILD OF EXILE

When Sālote was just two years old, her mother tragically died, and her father, George Tupou II, decided he had to remarry, so that he could have more children and secure his throne.

This placed his eldest daughter in terrible danger. Many of the noble families of Tonga didn't want Sālote to inherit the throne, some even saying it was traditional to kill the children of a first marriage. So, to protect her, George Tupou II sent Sālote to Auckland, in New Zealand.

She was only nine years old, but Sālote had to learn to cope with missing her family, and pray that one day she would be allowed to return.

HOMECOMING

Every Christmas, she was given a chance to come home for a short visit to celebrate with her father. But at New Year she had to leave Tonga for New Zealand, and continue her education.

She returned to Tonga as a teenager, and when she was just eighteen, decided to marry Viliami Tungī Mailefihi, the son of Tonga's prime minister. Their marriage brought together all three of the powerful royal lines of Tonga: the Tuʻi Tonga; Tuʻi Kanokupolu; and Tuʻi Haʻatakalaua. Sālote became queen later that year.

TIME TO RULE

Sālote took a great interest in preserving Tonga's history. But she soon realized her father had left the country in a lot of debt, and her people were divided and unhappy.

Then, in the first year of her reign, a terrifying global pandemic arrived on her island's shores.

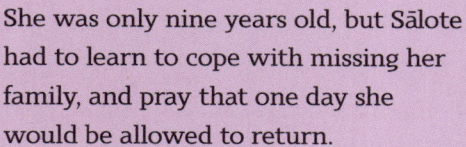

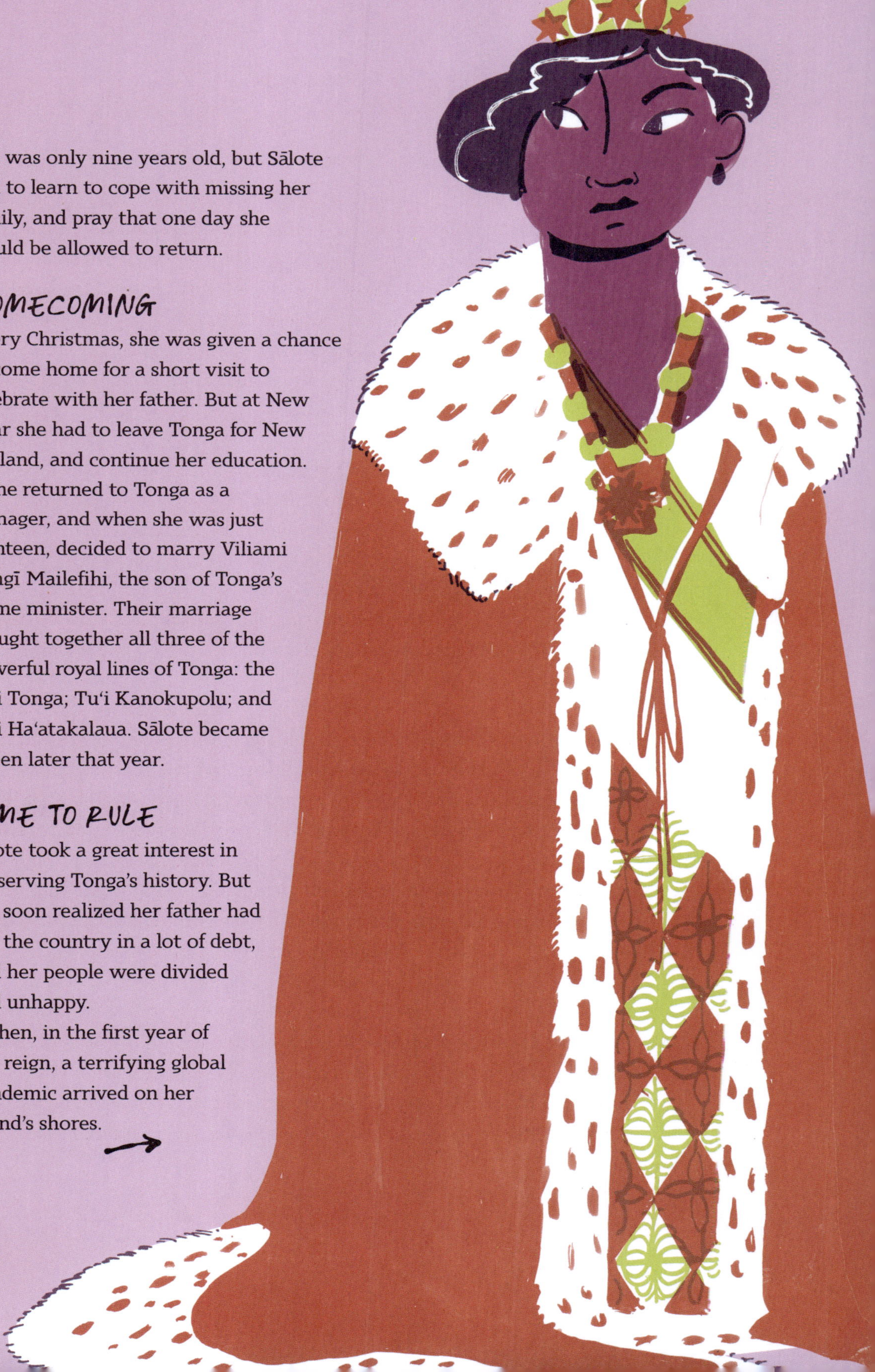

The Tongan flag was designed in the 19th century, becoming officially part of Tonga's constitution in 1875.

The Spanish flu had decimated Europe and the Americas, and soon it razed through Tonga as well. Entire families and villages were wiped out. It even killed members of the royal family, but Sālote survived.

BOLD AND BRILLIANT

Determined to help her people, Queen Sālote set up a Department of Health so that every islander could receive free healthcare. Then she set up a medical school to train doctors and nurses.

But Queen Sālote didn't stop there – moving on to advocate for education and supporting the campaign to give women the right to vote. Sālote believed men and women should be recognized as equal under British law, just as they were in traditional Tongan society.

Although she was only a young queen, Sālote's actions made her loved by her people. She was incredibly tall, at 1.9 m (6.25 ft), striking, and determined to protect her people's traditions.

Few people outside Tonga knew that she was also a talented poet, often setting her own words to traditional music and dance. She wrote vulnerable, powerful poems about loss and hope:

> "RAIN FALLING ON THE MOUNTAIN-TOP
> DESCENDS TO THE VALLEY OF SORROW
> FLOWING INTO THE OCEAN
> TURNING INTO BITTERNESS?"

DEFENDER OF ALL

In 1939, a new threat to Tonga appeared, as World War II reared its ugly head. Declaring war on Germany and the Nazis, Sālote and her government created the Tongan Defence Force. Nearly every single man in Tonga signed up, determined to help fight for the Allies.

Worried about the danger of invasion by Japan, Queen Sālote personally oversaw her country's defence. When the Japanese bombed Pearl Harbor, it was Tonga that stepped up to provide a home and base for American soldiers and sailors during their Pacific campaign. The British airforce even named a Spitfire plane "Queen Sālote" in her honour.

But even though Tonga fought bravely during World War II, they were often overlooked and forgotten. However, in 1953, Queen Sālote attended the coronation of Elizabeth II in London, and for the first time, her image was beamed onto televisions across the world. Suddenly everyone wanted to know who the noble and brave queen of Tonga was, and about the country she called home.

HER LEGACY LIVES ON

There was one thing left for Queen Sālote to do. She was determined that Tonga would be independent. Her dream came true in 1970, when Tonga was emancipated from British rule, free to decide its own fate once more.

GLOSSARY

Catholic church
A specific branch of Christianity. The head of the Catholic Church is the Pope, based in the Vatican.

Colonization
The act of taking over another country and its people, sometimes by moving lots of new people in and sometimes by running its government from a distance.

Duchy
The territory of a duke/duchess.

Dynasty
A royal family ruling an area from one generation to another.

Exile
When someone is forced to leave their home or country.

Galleon
A large sailing ship.

Heir
The person who is next in line to the throne.

Illegitimate
A person born of parents not lawfully married to each other and so who cannot be in the line of succession.

Protestant church
A specific branch of Christianity that separated from the Catholic Church in the 16th century.

Regent
A person acting as a leader on behalf of a ruler, often because the ruler is too young to rule.

Revolution
A change in a political, economic, or social system over a short period of time.

Shia
One of the two main branches of Islam.

Siege
A military operation to surround a city or fort to try and capture it.

Succession
Order in which members of a royal family become the next ruler.

Suffragette
A female activist who fought for women's right to vote, often using militant tactics.

Sunni
One of the two main branches of Islam. Sunni Islam is the largest branch of Islam.

Vizier
A title once given to a chief official in some countries.

INDEX

A
abdication 54, 57
Æthelred of Mercia 19, 21
Agnes of Bohemia, St 53
Ahmed el Outassi, Sultan 42–3
AIDS 39
Akbar the Great, Emperor 46–7
Albert of Saxe-Coburg and Gotha, Prince 65
Alexander II of Russia 64
Alfred the Great of Wessex 19
Ali al-Sulayhi of Yemen 22, 23
Al-Mukarram Ahmed 23, 24, 25
Amina of Zazzau 15
Anarchy, the 26
Anglo Saxons 19–21
Anne of Denmark 62
Anthony, Marc 11
Asaf Khan 47
Asante Empire 70–3
Asma of Yemen 22, 23

B
Bafena of Ethiopia 63
Barbarossa brothers 42
Basina, Princess 52
Boleyn, Anne 48
British Empire 71–3, 74, 77
Brown, John 65

C
Caesar, Julius 10, 11
Camulodunum 12
Catherine II the Great of Russia 29
Catholicism 48, 50
charity 7
Charles III of the United Kingdom 39
Charles of Blois 34
Charlotte of Belgium 63
Chauragarh Fort (India) 47
Ci'an, Empress Dowager 68
Clotilda, Princess 52
concubines 66
Crusades 31–2
Cyrus I the Great of Persia 52

D
Dalpat Shah 44–5, 46
Damasithymos of Calyndos 9
Dee, John 50
de Montfort, John 34, 35
Descartes, René 56
Diana, Princess of Wales 39
divorce 32, 48
Drake, Sir Francis 51

E
education 4, 10, 21, 36, 37, 55, 56, 75, 76
Edward VI of England 48, 50
Egypt, ancient 10–11
Elizabeth II of the United Kingdom 77
Este, Ercole d' 36
exile 53, 73, 74–5

F
Ferdinand I of Naples 36
Ferdinand II of Aragon 62

Forbidden City (China) 66–9
Frederick II, Holy Roman Emperor 53
Froissart, Jean 34

G
Garha, Kingdom of 44, 45, 46, 47
Geoffrey V of Anjou 27
George Tupou II of Tonga 74, 75
Golden Stool 71–2, 73
Gonzaga, Francesco, Marquis of Mantua 36, 37
Grey, Lady Jane 50
Guangxu Emperor 68–9
Gustav Adolphus of Sweden 54–5

H
Hastings, Battle of 26
Hastings, Lady Flora 64
healthcare 76
Hennebont, Siege of 35
Henry II of England 27, 32–3
Henry of Huntingdon 20
Henry V, Holy Roman Emperor 26
Henry VIII of England 48

I
Ibn Najah, Sa'id 23, 24, 25
Iceni 12
Irene of Greece and Denmark 53
Isabella I of Castile 62
Ismailism 22

J
James I of England (James VI of Scotland) 62
Japan, World War II 77
Joseph II, Holy Roman Emperor 60, 61

L
Lavinia of Tonga 74
Leonardo da Vinci 37
Livia Drusilla 28
Li Yuan (Emperor Gaozu) 16–17
Londinium 13
Louis VI of France 31, 32
Louis VII of France 31

M
Mantua 36–7
Margaret of Anjou 29
Maria Eleonora of Brandenburg 54, 55
Marie Christina, Duchess of Teschen 61

marriage, rejection of 4, 7, 10, 48–53
Mary I of England 48, 50
Massagetae people 52
Matilda of Tuscany 14
Mecca 23
Menilek II of Ethiopia 63
Mercia, Kingdom of 19–21
Michelangelo 37
monarchy, abolition of 53
Morocco 42–5
Mughal Empire 46–7
Myeongseong (Queen Min) 38

N
Nana Akwasi Afrane Okese 71
Nero, Emperor 13
Nile, Battle of the 10
Norman Conquest 21, 26

O
Octavian (Emperor Augustus) 11, 28
Odaenathus of Palmyra 14
onna-musha 15

P
Pacific Islanders 74
patrons 5, 6, 21, 36–7, 57, 62
Pearl Harbor 77
Persian Empire 8–9
Peter I the Great of Russia 59
Philip II of Spain 50, 51
Philip VI of France 34, 35
philosophy 6, 37, 56
pirate queens 8–9, 40–3
Plantagenet dynasty 33
poison 11, 66, 68, 69
Prasutagus of the Iceni 12
Prempeh I of the Asante 73
prisoners 11, 29, 32, 33, 50
Protestantism 48, 50
Ptolemy XIII, Pharaoh 10

R
Ranavalona I of Madagascar 38
Raymond of Poitiers 32
religion 21, 22, 23, 25, 48, 50
Romans 11, 12–13, 14, 28
Russo-Ottoman War 59

S
Salamis, Battle of 9
samurai 15
Sarman (elephant) 45–6, 47
Shia Islam 22, 25
Singorgarh Fort (India) 45

Sophia Duleep Singh, Princess 39
Spain, expulsion of Muslims and Jews 41, 42, 62
Spanish Armada 51
Spanish flu 76
Stephen of England 27
succession 28–9, 48, 68
suffragettes 39
Sunni Muslims 41

T
Tang dynasty 17
Tarakanova, "Princess" 29
Tettenhall, Battle of 20
Thirty Years War 56
tigers 45, 46
Titian 37
Tomoe Gozen 15
Tomyris of the Massagetae 52
Tongzhi Emperor (Zichun) 66, 68
Tower of London 50
Tungī Mailefihi, Viliami 75

V
Vatican 63
Verulanium, Battle of 13
Vikings 19–21
voting 6, 7, 8, 39, 76

W
warriors 6, 8–9, 12–17, 20, 33, 44–7
Wars of the Roses 29
Wessex, Kingdom of 19, 21
William I the Conqueror of England 26
World War II 77
writers 5, 6, 60
Wu Zetian 28

X
Xerxes I of Persia 8–9
Xianfeng Emperor 66

Y
Yangdi, Emperor 16, 17
Yemen 22–5

Z
Zenobia of Palmyra 14
Zewditu of Ethiopia 63

Editorial Vicky Richards, Carron Brown
Design and Additional Illustration Kit Lane
Managing Editor Penny Smith
Managing Art Editor Anna Hall
Production Editor Gillian Reid
Production Controllers Ben Radley, Inderjit Bhullar
Associate Publishing Director Francesca Young
Art Director Mabel Chan

The publisher would also like to thank Dr Kit Heyam for a sensitivity read, Professor Fozia Bora for additional consulting, Hazel Beynon for proofreading, and Helen Peters for the index.

First published in Great Britain in 2026 by
Dorling Kindersley Limited
20 Vauxhall Bridge Road,
London SW1V 2SA

The authorised representative in the EEA is
Dorling Kindersley Verlag GmbH. Arnulfstr. 124,
80636 Munich, Germany

Copyright © 2026 Dorling Kindersley Limited
A Penguin Random House Company
10 9 8 7 6 5 4 3 2 1
001–356082–Apr/2026

All rights reserved.
No part of this publication may be reproduced, stored in or introduced into a retrieval system, or transmitted, in any form, or by any means (electronic, mechanical, photocopying, recording, or otherwise), without the prior written permission of the copyright owner.
DK values and supports copyright. Thank you for respecting intellectual property laws by not reproducing, scanning or distributing any part of this publication by any means without permission. By purchasing an authorised edition, you are supporting writers and artists and enabling DK to continue to publish books that inform and inspire readers. No part of this publication may be used or reproduced in any manner for the purpose of training artificial intelligence technologies or systems. In accordance with Article 4(3) of the DSM Directive 2019/790, DK expressly reserves this work from the text and data mining exception.

A CIP catalogue record for this book
is available from the British Library.
ISBN: 978-0-2417-8985-8

Printed and bound in China.

www.dk.com

ABOUT THE AUTHOR

Dr Fern Riddell is a cultural historian. Presenter of Sky History's *Truthseekers*, and host of their podcast series #NotWhatYouThoughtYouKnew, she is the author of multiple books including *Death In Ten Minutes: The forgotten life of radical suffragette Kitty Marion* and *Victoria's Secret: The Private Passion of a Queen*.

As an on-screen expert and series consultant, Fern has appeared on documentaries for the BBC, ITV, Channel 4, Channel 5, Sky Arts, Sky History, Smithsonian, and Discovery+, and is an internationally recognized expert historian for both radio and television. Writing widely for the press, her work can be found in The Guardian, Huffington Post, Times Higher Education, the i, The Telegraph, Prospect Magazine, New Statesman, History Today, and BBC History Magazine.

ABOUT THE ILLUSTRATOR

Taylor Dolan was born into a house of stories and raised in Texas. Her mother used to read to her every night, and together they made their way through the worlds of Narnia, Oz, and many more. Sometimes, when Taylor is feeling blue, her mother still reads to her and does the best voices for all the characters.

She is a Trinity University alumnus, having graduated in 2012 with her bachelor's degree in Art. She went on to receive her master's degree at the Cambridge School of Art in Children's Book Illustration. She works as a full time illustrator and author on all sorts of exciting projects from re-illustrating classics like *The Phantom of the Opera* and *The Nutcracker* (The Folio Society) to writing and illustrating her own series *Ghost Scouts* (Guppy Books).